"

I am of old and young, of the foolish as much as the wise; Regardless of others, ever regardful of others, Maternal as well as paternal, a child as well as a man, Stuff'd with the stuff that is coarse, and stuff'd with the stuff that is fine; One of the Great Nation, the nation of many nations, the smallest the same, and the largest the same..."

—Walt Whitman, "Leaves of Grass" (1900)

Table of Contents

Introduction

This book is short. Intentionally so.

It's a simple guide for those who seek to replicate the magic of Silicon Valley in designing their own ecosystems.

Almost everything in this book comes from the "other" book, *The Rainforest*. But the "other" book is 304 pages long, and many of you have asked for something shorter. Like a beginner's manual. So we have distilled the information from the "other" book down to its practical essence. This is not a detailed roadmap, but it's a framework to get you started in building your own Rainforest. We plan to publish a more comprehensive *Rainforest Handbook* soon.

Over the past year, thousands of you have talked with us about the Rainforest. You are launching your own Rainforests all over the world. Watching this happen is humbling.

This *Rainforest Blueprint* applies to all forms of human organization, whether you're talking about a nascent startup of two, a massive corporation with 100,000 employees, or a city, state, or nation of millions.

The Rainforest model is universal because we are starting from first principles, to ask: what makes human beings tick? From there, we construct an entire model of how human organizations function, and how we can make them more productive. Thus, we connect the micro and the macro.

Decades ago, business guru W. Edwards Deming realized that human connectivity was the key to higher profits, better quality products, and more loyal customers. When we deconstruct what makes Silicon Valley tick, we find Deming. We also find great thinkers like Nobel laureates Ronald Coase (law and economics) and Elinor Ostrom (political economy), E.O. Wilson (sociobiology), AnnaLee Saxenian (regional planning), and Cass Sunstein (law), among many others.

We have deliberately kept this book concise. Thus, we don't address a lot of things. We don't talk much about the underlying scientific research, across many disciplines, that substantiates the Rainforest model. We don't talk much about scaling in a massively parallel way. We don't talk much about quantitative metrics. You can read about some of that in the "other" book. And we will keep updating our blogs, as we come up with more.

We are still learning. Our ideas are always in draft mode. We revise and improve with each insight, conversation, and revelation. We view this book as a conversation with you, our reader. Visit us on the web at www.t2vc.com, and let us know what you think. How do we make these ideas even better? How do we shift the global paradigm? How do we reinvent the entire way we govern nations, run companies, and manage economies?

This Rainforest movement belongs to you. We are grateful to have you with us, as we transform the way the world conceives value.

Keep remembering to dream, trust, and pay it forward...

—Victor W. Hwang and the Team at T2 Venture Capital

Selected photos in this book are drawn from our work,
including the Global Innovation Summit of July 2012 and
various Rainforest-building projects around the world.
Learn more at www.t2vc.com and www.innosummit.com

We teach skills and tools to create Rainforests in live design
workshops. You can become a certified Rainforest Architect.
Sign up at www.rainforest-architects.com

PART 01

The Foundation

A short introduction to the foundational structure of innovation ecosystems

Open the door.

This is a short, practical guide for changing the world. Whether you're in a startup, large corporation, university, government agency, investment fund, professional firm, development institution, civic organization, or practically anywhere else.

But unlike other manifestos, this one does not ask you to boil the ocean or move impossible mountains.

In fact, just the opposite.

You can change the world in discrete steps. One person at a time. One action at a time.

You matter.

This book is about how you live your life.
And how you affect others around you.

Done right, you can transform your world.

You can design, shape, and build the
ecosystem around you. In ways that create
new ideas, better solutions, and improved
quality of life.

Leave the building.
Enter the Rainforest.

Humans are biological animals, so our society is a biological system. Biological systems, like natural rainforests, thrive because of the unplanned, uncontrolled results of countless interactions among flora and fauna.

As a result, they adapt. They evolve.

It's similar for human beings. Our society, our networks, are a type of ecosystem too.

They are Rainforests, but made of people. Our world depends on the interactions of people who possess talent, capital, and ideas.

That means everyone.

Human ecosystems can thrive...

... when our behaviors, our culture, allow individuals to interact in countless, unplanned, uncontrolled ways conducive to the blossoming of new ideas, new solutions, and new ventures. There is often deep value lurking in what seems at first frivolous, messy, and surprising.

But what is the recipe to cause that type of unusual behavior? How do we nurture entire ecosystems of serendipity?

To know where we are going, we must first understand where we are coming from...

Innovation is not the same as productivity.

Since the dawn of the Industrial Revolution, we have assumed that value was created through controlled processes. Like a farm. Or an assembly line. And that is indeed how we *optimize* value. By making things faster, cheaper, and more consistently.

For example, on a farm, we know in advance the crop we want. And we strive to grow that crop as productively as possible. We try our best to control irrigation, fertilizers, and soil conditions. When weeds happen to appear, we kill them.

We apply the same mindset for all mass-produced goods. That is how civilization makes useful things so cheaply.

You wouldn't want someone on the iPhone assembly line to make your phone radically different from the others. You expect a working iPhone, just like all the other iPhones.

Innovations are like weeds.

Innovation is basically the opposite of mass production.
We don't want predictable crops. We want weeds.

And weeds are birthed from uncontrolled environments.
We call such places—like Silicon Valley—Rainforests.

Think about some of the hottest companies today: Facebook, Twitter,
Google. Not that long ago, these companies were like weeds. They were
little sprouts, and no one knew for sure if they would grow bigger. In
Rainforests, we seek to nurture the growth of weeds.

So we end up with this interesting paradox... **Plants are harvested most
efficiently on farms, but weeds sprout best in Rainforests.**

To grow Rainforests, instead of trying to count individual weeds or the
flowers they create, what matters is the quality of the soil. Flowers
come and go. Good soil, however, will sprout good weeds. And their
flowers will continue to bloom, season after season.

What causes weeds to flourish is what we can't see. The most important things in Rainforests— our mindsets, our culture—are invisible. The good news, however, is that mindsets can be changed. **Culture is free.**

Culture is the third lever of economics.

Economists have said for decades that there are only two basic levers to affect economic value.

- *Fiscal* decisions are about *what* we spend—which things do we allocate resources to?

- *Monetary* decisions are about *when* we spend—do we borrow from the future to spend in the present, or vice versa?

The Rainforest gives us a third lever... *culture*. Culture is shaped by *how* we spend. The right culture is what allows Rainforests to be built, from the bottom up, action by action, weed by weed.

The way we do something matters just as much as—if not more than—the fact that we do it.

The funny thing is, you already knew this intuitively. For example, *how* you run an elementary school impacts children beyond just having a schoolhouse. Obviously.

The same principle holds true for everything we do.

Trust = Growth

Here's another funny thing. It took a long time for the experts to figure it out, but they're reaching a similar conclusion. Scientists are accumulating insights scattered across many disciplines. If you fit the puzzle pieces together, like a symphony fits together a bunch of musicians, you can hear the whole music.

What is that symphony telling us? That you are more powerful than you ever realized. That the trust you build through your interactions with others can grow an entire Rainforest.

> **Mathematics** says humanity, despite its complexity, can be modeled and calibrated like a system. Little tweaks can make a big difference.

> **Physics** says the universe is not as deterministic as it appears on the surface. Which means that the system works because of you, not despite you.

> **Biology** says species thrive when they learn to cooperate in complex divisions of labor to solve problems. That humans can "cooperate to compete" so well is what sets us apart and has allowed us to flourish.

> **Psychology** says we are tribal creatures. We are hungry for community, but prone to distrust strangers. We do things for all sorts of seemingly irrational reasons.

> **Economics** says zero-sum games become positive-sum when people communicate better. Distrust and distance create transaction costs. The more we trust, the wealthier we become.

> **Law** says that unwritten rules are more powerful than written laws. Handshakes are more efficient than lengthy agreements. But while unwritten rules may guide our daily lives, they require a lot of trust.

> **Design** says value comes from the bottom up, and process determines output. Trust-based environments lead to better solutions. Fear-based mindsets lead to stagnation.

If you listen to the whole symphony, rather than the individual instruments, the music is clear. Trust equals growth. And your actions are what create that trust.

Every conversation changes the world.

For the longest time, most of us believed that business was business. That emotion didn't matter. That dispassionate, rational decision-making should dictate how we run organizations.

We were wrong.

We now realize that innovation comes not from raw economic ingredients, whether land, labor, capital, or technology. It comes from the recipe.

And that recipe is based on patterns of behavior at the individual level. That is, culture. Culture affects how efficiently people combine together to solve problems. This applies to all forms of economic activity: startups, incubators, corporate initiatives, mentoring programs, venture capital

funds, corporate venture funds, angel investor networks, university technology transfer offices, government programs, professional services, and on and on.

The way people interact at the micro level affects the system at the macro level. Even two people sitting in a coffee shop. Every conversation matters.

Can we transform culture?

In a word, yes.

But we don't transform culture by ordering people around. Or moving money from one pocket to another. Or constructing monuments to our own genius.

We change culture by starting at the foundation. We start with individuals. We build roots before branches.

To cultivate a Rainforest, you must become a designer. But this design process is special, because your medium is not a tangible one, like plastic, metal, cement, or paint.

Instead, your canvas is society. Your paintbrush is human nature.

PART 02

The Frame

Building your Rainforest can be divided into three steps.

**Seed.
Cultivate.
Nourish.**

Most of our lives we spend in **Cultivation**. We stay busy growing crops we are familiar with, maybe doing little tweaks here and there, but never straying too far from the parameters we know. We don't plant too many new **Seeds**. Nor do we enjoy the hard work of **Nourishing**. We are afraid of too much uncertainty, and we get bored with too much certainty.

So usually we inhabit the middle space.

When you build a Rainforest, you need to shake up the system and stretch people outside their comfort zones. You need to lead people to the left, where new ideas come from, where there is deep uncertainty.

You need to move them back to the middle, where ideas turn into actionable plans. Then you need to lead them to the right, where hard things get implemented, where there is serious risk of project abandonment.

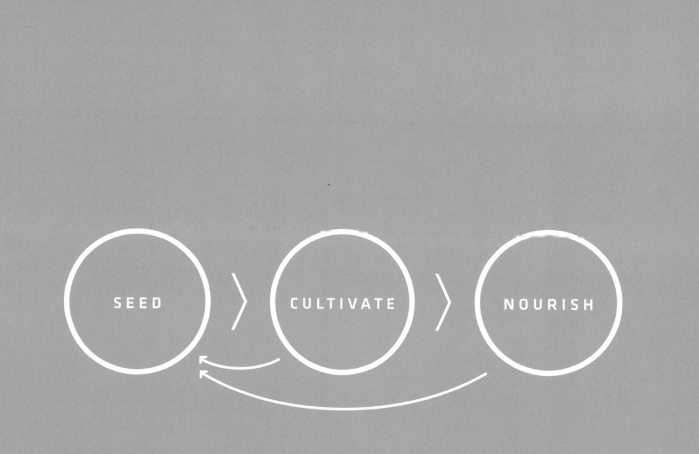

Step One.
Seed your Rainforest by generating fresh ideas.

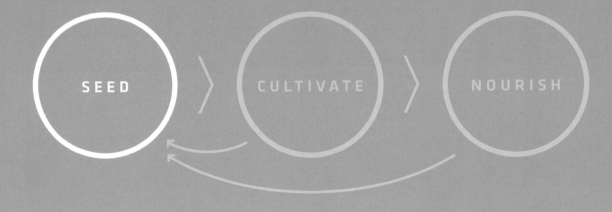

Analogy	*Loosen*
Mindset	*Divergent Chaos*
Process	*Design*
Tool	*Rainforest Canvas, Social Contract*
Output	*Idea Flow*
Success	*Solutions Generated*

Think of it like fixing a misaligned screw.

You loosen.
Calibrate.
Then tighten again.

If everything works, the result should be a better fit than you had before.

And the process never stops. Just as the shape of wood warps and changes the fit of a screw, the world keeps changing, too. So your Rainforest has to keep loosening, calibrating, and tightening.

Again and again.

1. First step...
Get your own self together.

Your ecosystem starts with you getting a grip on yourself.

Be aware of your real self, particularly your personal fears.

Do you feel threatened by others? What makes you insecure? When are you afraid of the unknown? Do you talk too much or bluster when you don't know what to say? Do you need status to make yourself feel important? Do you drop names to compensate for your own insecurities?

You are more transparent than you realize. Believe us, people know.

It's natural to be insecure. We are animals, too. And we are wired to protect ourselves, to fit in, to maintain our status, to fight for turf, to defend from threats.

But your fears are transmitted to those around you, and they drag down your ecosystem. They create fear in others. They make people stop talking and sharing with you, and each other. They freeze innovation.

You can't build a Rainforest if the foundation is unstable. And that foundation is *you*.

What to do about your crazy, imperfect self? Take some leadership training. Meditate and get to know yourself better. Ask your friends how you can do better. Make more jokes about yourself. Foster intimate relationships. Forgive the trespasses of others. Allow yourself a healthy cry. Focus on where you want to go, because that vision of the future can ease the pain of the past and the present.

Most of all, be authentic. That always wins in the end.

2. Convene people with influence across boundaries.

How do architects think?

When architects design a building, they don't just think about what's happening inside the building. They focus on how people move in and out of the building efficiently. Their overriding goal is to lower the barriers between people, whether inside or outside, and make it easier to connect.

Now think of doing that same task, but without the building.

That's your job when building a Rainforest. You need to foster the same connectivity in virtual space. And instead of dealing with physical constraints, as in a building, you must confront the social and psychological constraints of human beings.

Invite diverse strangers together.

People who are the most diverse have the most to gain from each other. Researchers have shown that a random group of diverse strangers can often solve problems better than a group of so-called experts. But diverse strangers are the least likely to meet on their own, because differences breed distrust. You must help overcome that in your Rainforest.

Focus on boundary crossers.

Identify people who span boundaries and build bridges between disparate individuals. Real-life linkages are human-to-human, not group-to-group. In biological systems, keystones are species—like bees and hummingbirds—who connect disparate parts of the ecosystem together. In your Rainforest, keystones create trust where there would otherwise be distrust. Thus, they can make value from nothing.

Invite people with genuine influence, not hollow titles.

Who is deeply respected as a human being? Whose opinion carries weight, regardless of their formal status? Who is regarded with the highest integrity? Get them in your founding team.

Physical space matters.

Environment shapes our behaviors, so pay attention to the physical setting. Are people meeting in the same location they associate with long, boring, useless meetings? Is the space warm and personalized, or cold and antiseptic? Does it make one happy or sad? Excited or tired? Shake things up. Change rooms. Borrow a room at another firm. Bring them to your house. Try a coffee shop.

3. Focus on process.
Because process = substance.

"Societies have always been shaped more by the media by which men communicate than by the content of the communication."

— **Marshall McLuhan and Quentin Fiore,**
The Medium is the Massage (1967)

Design thinking is a hot topic these days. At its core, the concept is quite simple. Environment affects output. Because it shapes the interactions between people and the things around them, for better or for worse.

How you convene your Rainforest matters. Your goal is to instill "creative confidence," as our friends at Stanford say. "Nudge culture, don't shove it." You have to make people comfortable enough to stretch outside their comfort zones. If they trust the situation enough, they will be more willing to "go there."

"Yes, and..."

Here are some simple tenets that designers often follow. You should make sure everybody in your Rainforest team understands these principles and agrees to follow them.

- **Listen actively.** Try extra hard to understand what others mean. Practice empathy. Be attuned to others' intentions.

- **Encourage the passions of others, rather than stifling them.** Save filtering for later. Instead of saying "no," say "yes and." Help everybody lay everything on the table. There are no bad ideas, just the early incarnations of good ideas. Let the ideas flow like water.

- **Make ideas tangible.** Express ideas with physical objects, rather than just verbal dialogue. It's like giving everyone an additional language. Designers often use lots of sticky notes, which make it easy to manipulate ideas around. But don't limit yourself. Let your imagination go. As designer John Maeda says, "Making a process visible makes a practice reflectable."

- **Bias towards action.** Don't just sit there and talk endlessly. Make stuff. Stack things. Draw. Write. Color. Do. Create something tangible as a group.

- **Try to use verbs, not nouns.** Nouns assume we know the answers already. Verbs, on the other hand, are freer because they focus on what we are doing and where we need to go. They allow us to reconstruct our own nouns, to solve the particular circumstances we are dealing with. Don't just buy "noun medicine" off the shelf. Make your own medicine.

4. Make it fun.

Joy, in all its incarnations, helps us overcome fear. Innovation is not a rational endeavor. It takes a lot of effort, risk, and likely failure. Without joy in the process, why bother?

It's the journey, not the destination.

Having fun also builds bonds and fond memories. Those help to launch your efforts with sufficient momentum to push through the inevitable bumps to come.

5. Write down your social contract. Sign it.

The unwritten rules of a Rainforest are its cultural code. They are the rules of engagement that govern how individuals, particularly strangers, work together on temporary projects to solve problems. They cause people to restrain their short-term self-interest for long-term mutual gain.

But you probably won't get someone like Moses coming down from the mountain with the code written on stone tablets. You have to make your own social contract explicit. By doing so, you make your culture tangible. You can literally make the invisible visible.

Each Rainforest has its own unique social contract, like every country has its own laws. When we deconstruct Silicon Valley, we find these fundamental Rules of the Rainforest constitute the underlying cultural code, like an unwritten constitution for its citizens:

Get the members of your Rainforest to develop their own social contract. It might be similar to the one on the right. Or it might be quite different.

Then get everyone to sign it. Physically. With a pen. Rituals unite people and help them remember their promises. They mark the passage from an old world to a new one.

Rule #1: *Break rules and dream.*

Rule #2: *Open doors and listen.*

Rule #3: *Trust and be trusted.*

Rule #4: *Experiment and iterate together.*

Rule #5: *Seek fairness, not advantage.*

Rule #6: *Err, fail, and persist.*

Rule #7: *Pay it forward.*

6. Give people toys to play with.

Toys make work livelier.

On the next pages is a toy we have created for you to use. We call it the Rainforest Canvas.

The Canvas is divided into blocks. Each block represents a critical piece of your Rainforest. They are interdependent, just like the flora and fauna in a natural rainforest. In order to get you started, each block has a few examples of the questions you might want to ask. However, you should not feel limited by what's in the boxes. Make the Canvas your own.

We'll keep a high-resolution version on our website. You can project the Canvas onto a wall. Or draw it on a whiteboard. Or anything you want. Then, let members of your Rainforest populate it. They can use sticky notes, dry erase markers, or whatever. Let people go at it.

If you have convened people in the right way, the results can be powerful. We have conducted Canvas workshops on five continents, and the results have been great every single session. People can literally see their Rainforest in physical form for the first time. It's amazing how people can live in a place for years without ever really seeing it.

The Rainforest Canvas

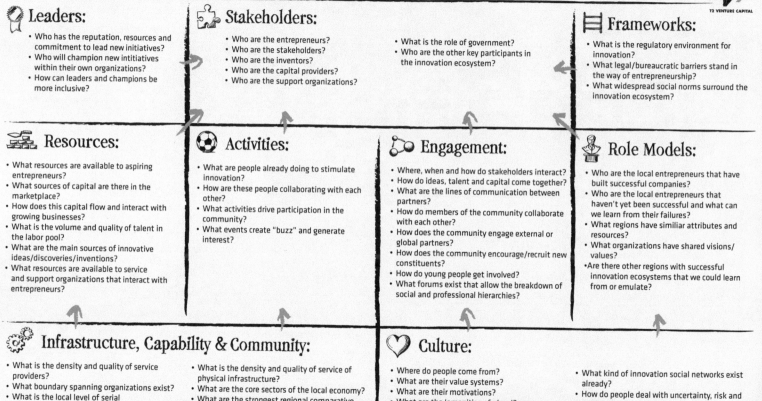

T2 VENTURE CAPITAL

Leaders:
- Who has the reputation, resources and commitment to lead new initiatives?
- Who will champion new intitiatives within their own organizations?
- How can leaders and champions be more inclusive?

Stakeholders:
- Who are the entrepreneurs?
- Who are the stakeholders?
- Who are the inventors?
- Who are the capital providers?
- Who are the support organizations?
- What is the role of government?
- Who are the other key participants in the innovation ecosystem?

Frameworks:
- What is the regulatory environment for innovation?
- What legal/bureaucratic barriers stand in the way of entrepreneurship?
- What widespread social norms surround the innovation ecosystem?

Resources:
- What resources are available to aspiring entrepreneurs?
- What sources of capital are there in the marketplace?
- How does this capital flow and interact with growing businesses?
- What is the volume and quality of talent in the labor pool?
- What are the main sources of innovative ideas/discoveries/inventions?
- What resources are available to service and support organizations that interact with entrepreneurs?

Activities:
- What are people already doing to stimulate innovation?
- How are these people collaborating with each other?
- What activities drive participation in the community?
- What events create "buzz" and generate interest?

Engagement:
- Where, when and how do stakeholders interact?
- How do ideas, talent and capital come together?
- What are the lines of communication between partners?
- How do members of the community collaborate with each other?
- How does the community engage external or global partners?
- How does the community encourage/recruit new constituents?
- How do young people get involved?
- What forums exist that allow the breakdown of social and professional hierarchies?

Role Models:
- Who are the local entrepreneurs that have built successful companies?
- Who are the local entrepreneurs that haven't yet been successful and what can we learn from their failures?
- What regions have similiar attributes and resources?
- What organizations have shared visions/ values?
- Are there other regions with successful innovation ecosystems that we could learn from or emulate?

Infrastructure, Capability & Community:
- What is the density and quality of service providers?
- What boundary spanning organizations exist?
- What is the local level of serial entrepreneurship?
- What is the density and quality of service of physical infrastructure?
- What are the core sectors of the local economy?
- What are the strongest regional comparative advantages?

Culture:
- Where do people come from?
- What are their value systems?
- What are their motivations?
- What are the 'amenities of place'?
- How do we create and maintain a sense of urgency?
- What kind of innovation social networks exist already?
- How do people deal with uncertainty, risk and randomness?
- How is failure perceived?
- Do people build for perfection or iteration?

The Rainforest Canvas

T2 VENTURE CAPITAL

Leaders:

Stakeholders:

Frameworks:

Resources:

Activities:

Engagement:

Role Models:

Infrastructure, Capability & Community:

Culture:

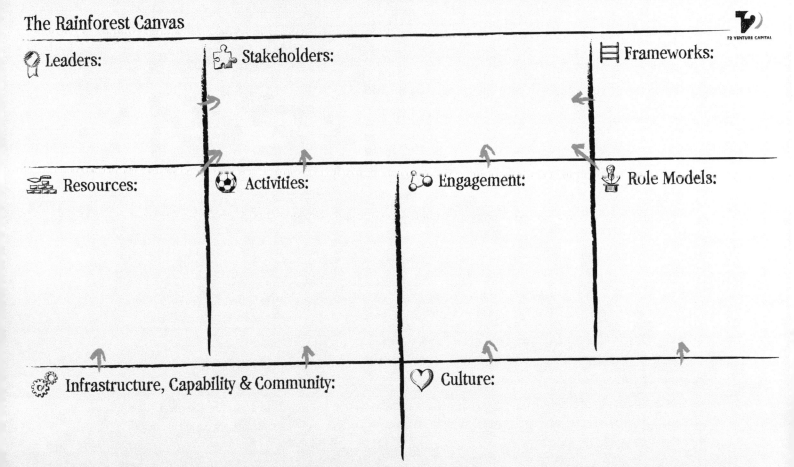

7. Focus on ways to bridge social divides.

As you fill out the Canvas, focus intensely on the bottlenecks in the social fabric of your Rainforest. Social barriers—caused by geography, networks, culture, language, and distrust—create transaction costs that stifle valuable relationships before they can be born. Above all else, you want to overcome those barriers.

- **Ask yourself, who is not collaborating with whom?** Are they not talking at all? Why not? How could you encourage those conversations? Who talks but still fails to communicate or bond? Why the distrust? Why the failed interactions? What's in the way?

- **Don't just focus inside the walls of your known Rainforest.** Look at outbound linkages, too. Those are the hardest to bridge. Who is far away, but critical to your Rainforest's health? The vibrancy of a Rainforest correlates to the number of people in a network, and there are far more people outside your current network than inside it.

- **You can often take an existing program and modify it,** so that it serves to bridge diverse social groups. That's much cheaper than creating something from scratch.

- **Modify incentive structures, so that people are rewarded for the behaviors you want.** Those behaviors might include following the social contract, creating positive-sum transactions, restraining short-term self-interest, or any number of other goals. Align people's incentives with the goals of the system.

Step Two.
Cultivate your Rainforest by turning the best ideas into actionable plans.

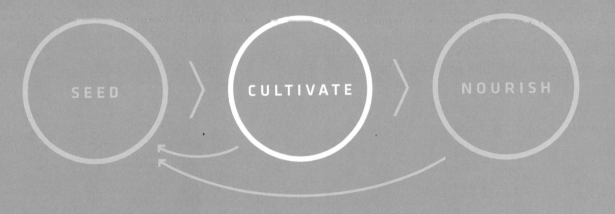

Analogy	*Calibrate*
Mindset	*Reflection*
Process	*Plan*
Tool	*Rainforest Tools, Rainforest Timeline*
Output	*Selected Actions*
Success	*Concrete Milestones*

It's time to start selecting ideas.

We have loosened, and now we must prepare to tighten.

Out of necessity, we need to separate the good from the bad. We only have so many hours in the day and so many dollars to spend. Chop!

We've all done action plans before. But if you're building a Rainforest, how does your team know what to keep and what to leave on the cutting room floor? How do you convert ideas into Rainforests?

1. Think like a shrink.

But instead of just changing one person's behavior, you are trying to change behaviors in a whole network of people. As therapists know, the most effective way to change people is through a process of real-world engagement, where they can personally experience the benefits of doing things differently. Over time, these activities lead to people learning new behaviors. New behaviors lead to changes in attitudes. And new attitudes eventually lead to changes in beliefs.

Behaviors > Attitudes > Beliefs

You can't change culture overnight. But you can create activities for learning. As your team selects which ideas you want to implement, focus on real-world programs that give people chances to discover new ways of doing things.

2. Build new trust networks by leveraging old trust networks.

How do you change people's thinking across vast networks, such as large organizations or regions?

The father of public relations, Edward Bernays, figured it out a century ago. People don't generally accept new ideas and behaviors by sheer logic or persistence. Instead, they change when people or institutions they already trust suggest so, whether explicitly or implicitly.

Think about the most trusted channels in your Rainforest. Which persons or institutions most command people's respect? Not respect based on fear or status, but based on who they are as human beings. You need to leverage those people or institutions. Recruit them to your Rainforest. Ask them to help. Leverage their credibility and trust to build something new.

3. Use the Rainforest Tools.

On the next two pages, we give you some guidelines for filtering ideas. These are what we call the Rainforest Tools. They are derived from the same methodology that therapists use to guide people's behaviors in constructive ways. Use these tools to help determine what ideas to keep, what to improve, and what to discard.

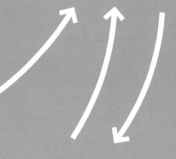

Event: Learn by Doing, Diversity

Cognitive Appraisal: Social Feedback, Social Contract *(Rules of the Rainforest)*

Behavior: Role Modeling, Peer-to-Peer Interaction

Emotion: Social Trust

Filter your ideas using these tools...

> **Tool #1: Learn by Doing.**
Seek ideas that nudge people into real-world activities, because that's how we learn to change.

> **Tool #2: Enhance Diversity.**
Seek ideas that cause people with highly diverse skills, backgrounds, networks, and insights to work together. This is hard, because the social fabric is weakest where people are the most different.

> **Tool #3: Celebrate Role Models and Peer Interaction.**
Seek ideas that leverage the channels people trust the most. We are usually influenced the most by successful role models and by peer validation.

> **Tool #4: Build Tribes of Trust.**
Seek ideas that cause the formation of groups where people will inherently trust one another more. Think of the power of university alumni networks or professional guilds. Consider creating new organizational networks for your Rainforest.

> **Tool #5: Create Social Feedback Loops.**
Seek ideas that help validate good behaviors and penalize bad behaviors. Social feedback loops are the carrots and sticks of human behaviors. Think of the power of eBay's star rating system. Now replicate that virtually in your Rainforest.

> **Tool #6: Make Social Contracts Explicit.**
Seek ideas that make the unwritten rules written. It's harder to follow the law if you don't know what it is.

4. Break down big ideas into little steps.

Start breaking down your big ideas into little steps, so you can build your Rainforest one discrete piece at a time. Assign roles and responsibilities.

And remember to keep having fun.

Here is another "toy" you can use: the Rainforest Timeline.

Convene your team. Project this timeline on the wall, or redraw it on a whiteboard. Let them go at it, manipulate it, play with it. Use sticky notes, markers, whatever artifacts fit the occasion. All the same design principles we talked about in Step One still apply: listen actively, encourage the passions of others, make ideas tangible, bias towards action, and try to use verbs instead of nouns.

And we'll post the electronic version on our website, for you to use freely.

Objectives	Tasks	Success Criteria	Timeframes	Resources	Stakeholders
What concrete action to build your Rainforest?	What smaller tasks to achieve objective?	What does success look like?	When do we need to achieve tasks?	What resources needed to achieve tasks?	Which stakeholder is responsible?
I.	A.	A.	A.	A.	A.
	B.	B.	B.	B.	B.
	C.	C.	C.	C.	C.
II.	A.	A.	A.	A.	A.
	B.	B.	B.	B.	B.
	C.	C.	C.	C.	C.
III.	A.	A.	A.	A.	A.
	B.	B.	B.	B.	B.
	C.	C.	C.	C.	C.

Step Three.
Nourish your Rainforest by experimenting, measuring, iterating.

Analogy	Tighten
Mindset	Convergent Certainty
Process	Implement
Tool	Rainforest Scorecard
Output	Precision Deployment
Success	Culture Change

Time to make things happen.

At first glance, Step Three of the Rainforest Blueprint looks like it might be like any other project implementation. Milestones, timelines, roles, responsibilities, blah, blah, blah.

But it's not the same.

True, your team needs to do all the things that a normal project implementation requires. You've got to do the work, after all.

But here's the twist...

What you *do* is not actually what you *measure*.

1. The hard stuff is soft.
The soft stuff is hard.

Business management guru W. Edwards Deming used to express this notion. Like him, we distinguish between the hardware and software of building Rainforests.

The hardware is the actual stuff you implement in building your Rainforest. It's the buildings, programs, money, labor, supply chains, distribution channels, marketing efforts, legal contracts, patent filings, and so on. Rainforests are full of lots of hardware. But you can have hardware—*like an empty building*—that is completely devoid of life.

The software is the stuff you can't see. It's the connectivity, diversity, joy, trust, social contract, and feedback loops in the system. They are absolutely critical, but they're almost impossible to see. And even harder to measure.

Below is a little diagram we devised to show the difference between hardware and software. If you want to dig in more deeply, check out the "other" book, *The Rainforest.* Even if you don't read the book, though, you can get the basic idea below just by looking at this diagram.

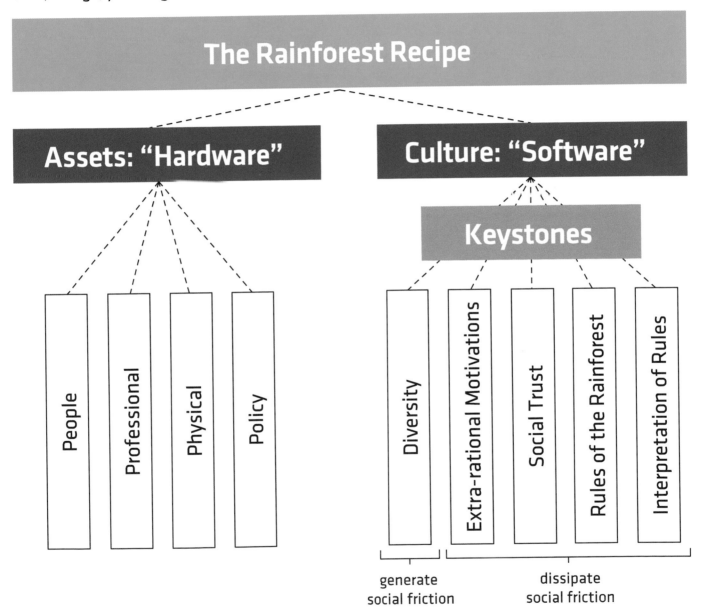

2. Do the what. Measure the how.

As you move into implementation, hardware tends to take over the brain. It's natural to focus on impending deadlines and budget targets when you have to get things done.

It takes extra effort to focus on the software. It's what Deming called "constancy of purpose." So to help you, we have created a tool to measure software. We call it the Rainforest Scorecard. It's a way of imposing discipline on the implementation process. This way, you won't lose track of the software while constructing the hardware.

Use this scorecard to grade the implementation of your Rainforest. We'll keep an electronic version on our website for you.

Rainforest Scorecard

On each row below, grade your Rainforest from 1 to 10, with 10 being highest.

Grading Period	1	2	3
Culture			
Trust is an important cultural element and is widespread and easily created.			
People think in terms of "positive-sum" or "win-win" situations and not "zero-sum" or "I win only if you lose"			
Failure is not viewed in a negative light.			
Calculated risk taking is viewed positively.			
People are often willing to help without expectation of immediate return.			
People are open with their time and knowledge.			
People are encouraged to dream and "think big".			
Average Grade x 3.5			
Leadership			
Who are the Rainforest's leaders? List as many as you can. Why are they leaders? Be specific.	*not scored*		
Overall, leadership promotes innovation.			
Leadership's perspective aligns with the perspective of others in the Rainforest working to promote innovation.			
Leadership comes from diverse backgrounds with diverse social, professional and cultural networks.			
Leaders are effective at communicating their visions and agendas to their constituencies.			
I understand the motivations of the Rainforest leadership.			
Average Grade x 2.5			

Frameworks, Infrastructure, Policies			
Stakeholders have strong communication channels and collaborations.			
Policies do not impede connectivity, trust, and collaboration.			
There are effective mechanisms of feedback where different stakeholders can learn from each other.			
Average Grade x 1			

Resources			
It is easy to access capital for deserving ideas.			
Up to date, relevant, and current information across a broad spectrum of disciplines is accessible by the majority of the Rainforest.			
The Rainforest's workforce is highly diverse and talented across a broad range of relevant skill sets that align with market demands.			
There are effective entrepreneurial resources, including experienced mentors to support new entrepreneurs.			
There are programs that specifically train workers to be current in their field, and these programs are widely accessible.			
Average Grade x 1			

Activities and Engagement			
There are numerous activities that actively promote connectivity and trust.			
These activities are effective in promoting new ideas, solutions, and products.			
These activities span a large spectrum of both technical domains and promote collaboration across diverse audiences.			
These programs have a high degree of engagement among diverse groups of participants.			
There are effective means of developing new high engagement activities in the Rainforest.			
Average Grade x 1			

Role Models			
Successful entrepreneurs are celebrated as role models in the Rainforest.			
Role models are actively engaged in supporting new entrepreneurs through a variety of means.			
Role models are widely known in the Rainforest.			
Formal recognition is given for innovative contributions to the Rainforest.			
There are systems to recognize and support high-potential future role models.			
Average Grade x 1			

SUM OF AVERAGES ABOVE (100 POSSIBLE)			

3. Watch for falling egos.

As you transition from Step One (Seed) to Step Two (Cultivate) to Step Three (Nourish), there is a subtle but profound shift in mindsets that should happen in your Rainforest.

Step One, the beginning of the process, was about letting personal dreams burst forth. Step Three, the implementation, is about realizing a common dream with others.

Therefore, the process of building a Rainforest should change people's way of thinking... **from finding community in their personal passions, to finding personal ways to implement a community vision.**

If you see that happening, you'll know you're on the right track. Watch for it.

WATCH FOR FALLING EGOS

4. Fail fast and cheaply.

Remember that there are never perfect answers. The world is complex and evolving. There will be lots of mistakes in your Rainforest.

But mistakes don't define us, they refine us.

Even failures are fine. When building Rainforests, failure is just a way of learning. Of course, failure stinks. But don't let fear of failure win.

Allow yourself to make lots of little failures. It's easier to fail in small, incidental ways than in big, dramatic ways. Thomas Edison tested over 2,000 materials before finding a functioning light bulb.

Adopt the same mindset in growing your Rainforest.

5. Play again.

If things don't work out right—and things will definitely not work out right—go back to Step One.

Adapt. Reload. Improve.

And try again.

Epilogue

In the end, it's pretty simple.

Technology, capital, startups, patents, incubators, research, universities... they're just physical manifestations of underlying value. To build a Rainforest, it all boils down to one thing.

All you need is... love.

Love is not some fuzzy thing. It drives innovation. As Harvard psychologist Steven Pinker describes, love is an extension of faith to another, where "the line of credit is long and the terms of repayment forgiving." It is what brings people together, makes them stretch beyond their usual comfort zones, and allows them to trust each other enough to take a chance and build something novel together.

Love is particularly important when trust is low, when people are different, when barriers are high.

So, keep love in mind. Spread it to others. Your Rainforest will grow.

Join us!

1. Tell us about your Rainforest. Send us feedback at www.t2vc.com.

2. Sign up for our newsletter. Get the latest insights.

3. Become a Rainforest Architect. Gain skills, tools, and a global peer network.

4. Be part of our Summit and workshops.

"Men go forth
to marvel at
the heights of
mountains and
the huge waves of
the sea, the broad
flow of the rivers,
the vastness of the
ocean, the orbits
of the stars, and
yet they neglect
to marvel at
themselves."

– Saint Augustine of Hippo,
Confessions, Book X, Chapter
VIII (397-398 A.D.) (as
translated by Albert C. Outler)

Man and Nature
Photo by the author,
while writing this book
Santa Cruz Beach,
March 7, 2013

Thanks

Watching the Rainforest movement grow, like a vibrant weed, has been a thrill. Our first Summit attracted delegates from 49 countries seeking to grow their own Rainforests. Over the years, we have worked with friends in numerous emerging Rainforests, including (in no particular order) Italy, Kazakhstan, Siberia (Russia), New Mexico, Nigeria, Atlanta, Saudi Arabia, El Paso and Ciudad Juárez (Texas and Mexico), various regions in Mexico, the European Union, various regions of New York State (Saratoga, Oswego, Stony Brook), Taiwan, Chicago, Bogotá and Medellín (Colombia), Armenia, Hong Kong, Austin, Japan, Porto Alegre (Brazil), Palestine, Western Michigan, Dorchester County (Maryland), Antofagasta (Chile), Ahmedabad (India), Singapore, Canada, and Egypt, among others. Apologies for not listing everyone.

Countless individuals have contributed to this book and the Rainforest community. We can't fit all of them here. The team at T2, past and present, are the core: Greg Horowitt, Henry Doss, Al Watkins, Ade Mabogunje, Alistair Brett, Janet Crawford, Scott Gillespie, Mark Newberg, Jason Steiner, Cecilia Moreno, Susan Brooksbank, and Eliot Peper, among others. In addition to the people mentioned in the original Rainforest book, we also want to thank those who have contributed in the past year, whether as book reviewers, conference participants, new Rainforest Architects, or in other ways. Thanks to Shaukat Abdulrazak, Lisette Acevedo, Gerald Ada, Olusola Adeola, Pallav Agrawal, Abdulaziz Al-Hargan, Abdallah Al-Najjar, Julie Alsing, Ghada Amer, Saad Andary, Erlinda Arriola, Nick Ashburn, Philip Auerswald, Helena Backes, Norman A. Bailey, Lisa Baird, Eric Ball, Jorge Barba, Paul Basil, Chee Yang Beh, Daniela Benavente, Rich Bendis, Angelika Blendstrup, Chris Bloom, Gary Bolles, Sean Boykevisch, Joe Bradley, Keely Brandon, Ned Breslin, Dennis Brobson, Juan Cano-Arribi, Bogdan Ceobanu, Rachel Chan, Jeffrey Char, Al Chase, Aditya Chinnareddy, Claudia Chittim, Megan Clark, Jeni Clark, Brandon Cohen, Bill Colglazier, Jason Collins, Rita Colwell, Miles Contreras, Johnson Cook, Gerardo Corrochano, Peter Coy, Adiba Cremonini, Christopher Croupe, Nitin Dahad, Carol Dahl, Marc Dangeard, Alberto de Palacio Hinojosa, Alex Dehgan, Gianluca Dettori, Krista Donaldson, Sue Dorsey, Tim Draper, Daniel Driscoll, Tania Dutta, Patricia Echeverria Liras, Odo Effiong, Nawsheen Elaheebocus, Fernando Fabré, Nina Fedoroff, Hernán Fernández Lamadrid, Dylan Fiesel, John Forge, Bob Frank, Katie Camille Friedman, Beatrice Gakuba, Diana Galperin, Susana Garcia Robles, David Gibson, Leon Glover, Simon Goldbard, Daniel Goldman, Paula Goldman, Bernadette Goovaerts, Bijoy Goswami, Jonathan Gotschall, Colin Graham, Shiv Grewal, Phillip Griffiths, Jeffrey Grimshaw, Mark Grobmyer, Carlos Guaipatin, Ossama Hassanein, Keasha Haythe, Geoffrey Helt, Al-Hassan Hleileh, Marty Howell, Jose Huitron, Rebeca Hwang, Arturo Iglesias, Rebecca Jackson, Bruce Jenett, Nancy Johnson, Edward Jung, Robert Kadar, Renee Kaplan, Sotiris Karagiannis, Evelin Kasenõmm, Gerry Kay, Elena Kaye, Randall Kempner, Maurice Kent, Islam Khalil, Nour Khrais, Bobby Kia, Jason Koenig, Christopher Koh, Michael Korver, Sean Kottke, Stanley Kowalski, Thane Kreiner, Kiyoshi Kurokawa, Eric Kutner, Elizabeth Kuuttila, Christopher Laing, Bruno Lanvin, Mark Lautman, Burton Lee, Alan Leshner, Tom Lorenz, Nancy Lowery, Maryanne McCormick, Kirsten McGregor, Lesil McGuire, Kate McKeown, Emma McKinstry, Michael Madison, Kanetaka Maki, Leonardo Maldonado, Francisco Manrique, Jose Cesar Martins, Ramesh Mashelkar, Nola Masterson, Wendy Matheny, Damon Matteo, Mark Mavroudis, John May, Chinenye Mba-Uzoukwu, Micha Mikailian, Henry Miller,

Lee Milstein, Neha Misra, Lesa Mitchell, Atsushi Mizushima, Andrea Moser, Marjan Moshref, Romain Murenzi, Burton Mwamila, Koichiro Nakamura, Hugo Nava, Juan Carlos Navarro, Audra Nemir, Kevin Neuberger, Ca Tran Ngoc, Rogelio Nochebuena, Katherine Noesen, Alistair Nolan, Eric Norman, Shig Okaya, Elinor Ostrom, Rena Pacheco-Theard, Flora Painter, Michael Partsch, Kevin Pen, Katie Petersen, Tom Pfaff, Dirk Pilat, Jim Pooley, Sandra Porras, Todd Porter, Tom Post, Diego Prieto, Sheena Pulapaka, Cindy Quezada, Pamela Quin, Deron Quon, Gayathri Radhakrishnan, Jorge Ramos, Mahendra Ramsinghani, Kevin Ready, David Reichbaum, Bill Reichert, Mario Reyes, Pete Richerson, Walter Rivera, David Rolf, Eric Rosenthal, Francisco Sagasti, Richard Samans, Boukary Savadogo, AnnaLee Saxenian, Anatoly Scherbakov, Mila Schilders, Will Schmitt, Shelby Schneider, Mario Scuderi, Justin Setzer, Rohit Shukla, Mike Sigal, Anton Silinin, Peter Singer, Bernard Slede, Frederick Smith, Neeraj Sonalkar, Agnes Soucat, Hammans Stallings, David Strangway, Cathy Swain, Natalie Sweeney, Jiro Tanaka, Shivam Tandon, Emily Tavoulareas, Andrew Taylor, Tuba Terekli, Chad Thacker, Cassandra Thomassin, Soody Tronson, Nuria Trujillo, Donna Tumminello, Larry Udell, Katie Updike, Hayato Urabe, Vivek Wadhwa, Richard Wallace, Walter Wang, George Warner, Takumi Watanabe, Michael Webber, Cary Westin, Phil Wickham, David Sloan Wilson, Florence Wong, Kwai Merng Woo, Zaahira Wyne, Heng Yang, Ting Ye, Christopher Yu, Jason Yuen, and Sofia Zabolotskih.

Thanks to Bill Rogers, for his amazing graphic design collaboration on this book.

To my parents, C.J. and Betty, I can never express enough love for the amazing gifts you've given me. To my mother-in-law, Angela, you have my deepest admiration and affection. To my wife, Christina, you are the crème to my brûlée, the dance to my drums, the love of my life. To my beloved sons, Anders and Augustine, you are the reason I do everything. Someday, you'll understand.

Credits

Page 3. Library of Congress, Prints & Photographs Division, NYWT&S Collection, cph.3c19650, from *Wikimedia Commons*, May 7, 2013, http://commons.wikimedia.org/wiki/File:V-J_Day_Times_Square_NYWTS.jpg

Page 6. Photographs by Don Mirra and Charles Mujie.

Page 16. Library of Congress, Prints & Photographs Division, LC-USW33- 059641, from *Wikimedia Commons*, May 7, 2013, http://commons.wikimedia.org/wiki/File:Airacobra_P39_Assembly_LOC_02902u.jpg

Page 19. Engraving from Mechanic's Magazine (cover of bound Volume II, Knight & Lacey, London, 1824). Courtesy of the Annenberg Rare Book & Manuscript Library, University of Pennsylvania, Philadelphia, USA, from *Wikimedia Commons*, May 7, 2013, https://commons.wikimedia.org/wiki/File:Archimedes_lever.png

Page 22. Giovanni Boldini, *Conversation at the Café* (1877-1878). Private collection. Painting - oil on panel, from *Wikimedia Commons*, May 7, 2013, http://www.wikipaintings.org/en/giovanni-boldini/conversation-at-the-cafe

Page 23. Si Griffiths, *Artist's Paint Brushes Adapted With Photoshop.* Surrey UK. 26 February 2005, from *Wikimedia Commons*, May 7, 2013, http://commons.wikimedia.org/wiki/File:Artist%27s_Paint_Brushes_Adapted_With_Photoshop._Surrey_UK.jpg

Page 30. Makklay, Tevaprapas. Phra Ajan Jerapunyo-Abbot of Watkungtaphao in Sirikit Dam. 2010. Location: Sirikit Dam Thailand. From *Wikimedia Commons*, May 7, 2013, http://commons.wikimedia.org/wiki/File:Phra_Ajan_Jerapunyo-Abbot_of_Watkungtaphao..jpg

Page 33. Scott Doorley and Scott Witthoft, *Make Space* (Wiley: 2013), 158.

Page 36. Gebhard Fugel, *Moses receiving the tablets*, c. 1900, from *Wikimedia Commons*, May 7, 2013, http://commons.wikimedia.org/wiki/File:Gebhard_Fugel_Moses_erh%C3%A4lt_die_Tafeln.jpg

Page 37. Alan Chia, *A pile of Lego blocks, of assorted colours and sizes.* 1 December 2007, 23:01, from *Wikimedia Commons*, May 7, 2013, http://commons.wikimedia.org/wiki/File:Lego_Color_Bricks.jpg

Page 45. Biser Todorov, *Tools.* 26 June 2010, from *Wikimedia Commons*, May 7, 2013, http://commons.wikimedia.org/wiki/File:Rusty_tools.JPG

Page 46. Adapted from a diagram in Jesse H. Wright, M.R. Basco, and M.E. Thase, *Learning Cognitive-Behavior Therapy: An Illustrated Guide* (Washington: American Psychiatric Publishing, 2006), 5.

Page 51. Ronald Saunders. Taken in Leigh NW England. This was once a prosperous furniture warehouse, now just an empty shell alongside the Leeds-Liverpool Canal. 31 March 2012, from *Wikimedia Commons*, May 7, 2013, http://commons.wikimedia.org/wiki/File:Flickr_-_ronsaunders47_-_WAS_YESTERDAYS_THRIVING_COMMERCE...jpg

Page 58. Adapted from Daan Verbiest, *Kangaroo Sign*, http://www.sxc.hu/photo/807208

Page 61. Steven Pinker, *How the Mind Works* (Norton: 1997), 507.

The Author

Victor W. Hwang is a venture capitalist and entrepreneur living in Silicon Valley. His firm, T2 Venture Capital, builds startup companies and the ecosystems that grow them. T2VC leverages the practical know-how of company-building to transform companies, organizations, and communities to become more innovative. The firm has served dozens of clients, such as the World Bank, USAID, and numerous governments and corporations on six continents.

Victor has founded or been involved in the original teams of several startup companies, including Liquidity Corporation (water purification), Veatros (digital search), and Blue Planet Strategies (copper production). He is the former President of Larta Institute, which accelerates the growth of hundreds of startup companies for federal research agencies each year. He practiced law as a corporate attorney on transactions ranging from angel and venture investments to multi-billion dollar corporate mergers and public offerings.

Victor is Executive Director of the Global Innovation Summit, a conference on building innovation ecosystems. He is primary author of the book *The Rainforest: The Secret to Building the Next Silicon Valley* and a contributing columnist to *Forbes*.

He received a bachelor's degree with honors from Harvard University. He received a law degree from the University of Chicago.

Made in the USA
Lexington, KY
26 August 2013